Darla's Dreamland

Written by Erlinda Zabella
Illustrated by Michael Noronha

Global Publishers Canada Inc.

Darla's Dreamland
Published by
Global Publishers Canada Inc.
1155 Midland Avenue, Suite 512
Scarborough, ON
M1K 4H3 Canada
Website: www.globalpublishers.ca
ISBN: 978-0-9865972-0-6
Printed in Canada

Darla's Dreamland

On a peaceful, enchanted island in the Philippines, there lived a little girl by the name of Darla. She lived on this beautiful island with her parents and her brother Ben, who was two years younger. Both of them loved to play outside on this warm and exotic island. Ben especially liked to spend his time playing in the meadows and the lush forests.

One Saturday morning, Darla and her brother Ben woke up early. They started doing their usual chores. Ben had to make the wooden floor shine, by scrubbing it with a coconut husk; he also had to help feed the animals in the barn. Ben liked animals. He often spoke to them. He loved all of them, but was particularly fond of a horse he named Eagle. Ben found him sick and weary when he was just a young colt. He guessed that Eagle must have been lost in the woods. Since then, he had taken care of the foal and nursed him back to health. Now, Eagle was a big, strong horse. Ben had even ridden on his back a couple of times.

Darla had to make the beds, dust the furniture, and water the plants. She loved to see them bloom. She thought the flowers in her house were so beautiful and had the sweetest smell. They were just about finished when mom called.

"Darla, Ben, come to the kitchen! Breakfast will be ready soon!"

"What is for breakfast mom?" Darla asked politely.

"We are having fried fish and rice, chocolate milk and ripe papaya. Hurry up now kids, before your foods get cold."

"That sounds good," Ben replied. "Fried rice and fish are my favorite foods for breakfast."

While they were eating, Ben noticed that his dad was not there. "Mom, where is dad?"

"Oh! Dad has headed out early to the fields. He said that the vegetables are ready, and the bananas, papayas and other fruits are ripening. Maybe I could sell some at the market today."

"You are going to the market today mom?" Darla was clearly very excited. "Can you buy me that red heart shape fruit that I ate at Uncle Sam's house? --- Oh! And some chocolate! --- And those little round fruits that come in a bunch! --- And ..."

"Sorry Darla," interrupted mom. "Those fruits are too expensive. Besides, we have lots of fruits. Why not have some of them instead?"

"But mom, we eat the same fruit everyday. Papayas and bananas, all the time. Besides, I like the fruit I had at Uncle Sam's house better."

Darla paused as she tried to remember the names of the strange fruits she had at Uncle Sam's house.

Suddenly she exclaimed "I remember now! They are called apples --- and grapes. They really are yummy."

"Alright" said mom, "I'll see what I can do."

"Yippee! Yippee! Hear that Ben? Mom is going to bring home apples and grapes." Darla was really beaming with joy.

"Yes, I heard you loud and clear," replied Ben with a teasing smile. "Goodness gracious! You don't have to jump around like a kangaroo. Besides, those fruits are not that delicious. I would take bananas and papayas over your apples and grapes."

"You little rascal! Here, have some more bananas and papayas, since you love them so much!" replied Darla who was a little bit annoyed at her brother.

"You two stop those silly arguments." Mom said in a stern voice.

"Yes mother," said Darla and Ben. Quietly they continued eating their breakfast.

"By the way, where do those fruits come from mom?" asked Ben.

"I know, I know!" exclaimed Darla who got excited again. "In Canada, or in any other country in the west. Uncle Sam told me that they grow in abundance. It would be nice, if we could go there someday." Darla closed her eyes. "Imagine all those delicious fruits, chocolate bars, stylish clothes, it must be paradise, it must be ..."

"Hey Darla, stop dreaming!" Ben poked her on the shoulder. "Don't forget, it's Saturday today and we planned on meeting our friends and going to the woods near the river. We can catch fish, pick some flowers, play with our kites, or go swimming. We can also take turns riding on Eagles back."

"You two, stop talking and finish your breakfast." interrupted mom. "By the way, if you are going to ride Eagle, make sure you stay in the meadow. Don't make that horse go too fast, and don't go very far."

"Yes mom." they both replied.

After they finished their meals and cleaned themselves, they were ready to go outside for the day.

Darla and Ben met with their friends on their way to the woods. They walked merrily along the path and through the bush as they discussed what they all should do first.

"We should go fishing!" exclaimed their friend Jesse.

"No, let's fly kites!" announced Annetta

"No, let's ride on Eagle's back!" proclaimed Ben.

This playful debate went on and on when suddenly Darla stopped.

"What's the matter Darla?" they all asked.

"I just thought of something. Uncle Sam said he was going to give me the magazines and postcards Aunt Lucia and his daughter Christina have sent him. You go ahead. I'll just stop by his house to pick them up. I'll catch up with you in the woods," and off she went. The other children just shook their heads and continued heading for the woods. Within seconds, they were chatting again.

It didn't take long for Darla to reach Uncle Sam's house and she quickly found herself in front of his door. She was just about to knock, when she saw him sitting under a big mango tree in his yard. On any other occasion, she would have noticed how lovely the mango trees were, with the branches so full of fruit. But not now. Darla hardly even noticed them at all.

"Uncle Sam!" Darla called. "Uncle Sam!"

"Right here Darla! Over here!"

"Good morning, Uncle Sam." Darla greeted politely. Right away she noticed the magazines and postcards in his hands. "Are those the magazines and postcards you promised me?"

"Good morning Darla. You are so early. I didn't expect you this early," replied Uncle Sam.

"My friends and I were heading for the woods. I thought that it would be nice to drop by now and catch up with them later. Then I could show my friends the magazines and postcards too. Isn't that a bright idea?"

"Yes! Yes, come and sit down. Here are the magazines and postcards and also a picture of Christina. It was taken during her last modeling session."

Darla looked eagerly at the photograph. "She is so gorgeous Uncle Sam!" Darla exclaimed, "And her dress...It is so pretty! It must be expensive."

"Not really. You see, as a model, she gets her clothes for free. She earns her own money as well," explained Uncle Sam.

"Wow!" cried Darla. "Canada must really be a dreamland." 'Not like where I am now.' Darla found herself thinking. 'I don't have nice clothes or the money to buy an apple.' All of a sudden Darla felt very sorry for herself.

"Hey, what's the matter?" Uncle Sam noticed that Darla looked sad.

"Oh, it's nothing. Anyway, I have to go. My friends must be wondering about me by now. Thanks for the magazines and postcards, uncle Sam."

"Before you go, there's something else I would like to tell you. I might be leaving for Canada soon. Aunt Lucia sent me a telegram. If you wish, you and Ben could come."

"What? Ben and I can come with you? I can finally go to Canada?" Darla could hardly believe what she had heard. Her heart lit up with joy.

"If you wish," said Uncle Sam, "and if your mother and father approve."

"Yes, Uncle Sam. You just don't know what this means to me!" Darla's heart was as light as a cloud.

Darla felt excited and nervous that entire day. She could hardly wait for mom and dad to come home. She didn't even mention the news to Ben. Instead she would look to the west where the sun set everyday. "I wonder what mom, dad, and Ben would think?" she asked herself.

When mom and dad finally arrived, Darla waited patiently until everybody settled in the living room. She kept looking at her mom and dad, who kept looking at each other as if they had something exciting to say.

Darla could sense something important was about to happen. Only Ben seemed not to notice. He was too busy painting.

Finally, mom broke the silence and said: "Darla, Ben, come closer. Your dad and I have something to tell you."

"Uh-Oh," Darla thought. "I wonder if this is what I think it's about?" She sat nervously in front of her mom and dad.

"What is it mom?" Ben asked.

"Darla," began her mother. "Your dad and I know how much you would like to go to Canada. Your Uncle Sam has been telling us lots of stories about it. That it is a very rich and beautiful country, right Darla?"

"Right mom." replied Darla.

"Well, your dad and I gave it a lot of thought and ..." Mom trailed off. She looked at dad, paused and drew a deep breath as she continued. "We've decided that we will go and find out for ourselves. It will be a big change for all of us, but we think it is worth a try, so what do you say kids?"

The children could hardly speak. They couldn't believe their ears. For a while they were tongue-tied. Darla was the first to break the silence.

"Oh mom," Darla jumped up for joy. "You just don't know how happy I am!"

"What about you, young fellow? What do you say?" Asked Dad.

Ben didn't answer. He just sat silently, staring at the floor.

Ben looked at mom. Tears started to form in his eyes. "Dad, I don't want to go to Canada. I am afraid, besides all my friends are here. We have fun together. And what about Eagle? I'll miss him so much. Please dad, I don't want to go."

Dad looked at mom, and then looked at Ben. "We are sorry Ben. Everything has already been arranged. We are all set to go."

"What about our house, the animals and the farm? Who will take care of them?"

"We thought of all those things before hand," replied dad. "Don't worry. Everything is well taken care of. With regards to Eagle, your cousin Ferdinand will be glad to take care of him while we're gone."

"It's all your fault, Darla. You and Uncle Sam. You don't care about our life here, the meadows and the woods. All you could think of are apples, grapes and fancy clothes. What's so good about them anyway?"

Crying, Ben stood up and ran to his room. Mom followed him, and tried to comfort him. In a soothing voice she kept telling him that everything was going to be okay --- that there is no reason to be afraid --- that life would be better in Canada. She stayed with him until he was calm.

That night everybody went to bed with a lot on their mind. They couldn't sleep. Mom and dad kept talking. Darla kept looking out the window. Ben didn't know what to think. He had mixed feelings. Finally, at around midnight, the house was quiet.

The days that followed were no ordinary days for Darla and Ben. They were kept very busy preparing to leave for Canada. Darla let everybody know that she would be leaving soon and that she would miss them all.

Ben was quieter that usual. He spent most of his time in the meadows with Eagle or drawing and painting in the woods.

One day, as he was drawing something, Darla approached him. "That's beautiful Ben. Can I join you?"

Ben didn't answer. He just frowned at Darla.

"Ben, I know you're mad at me," said Darla as she sat beside him. "I know you love your life here. I love this place too Ben, but you have to think of it this way. It is a chance for all of us to have a better life. For mom and dad who have been working in the fields for most of their lives. You do understand, don't you Ben?"

"Perhaps --- Maybe --- I don't really know." Ben said quietly as he continued drawing. Suddenly Ben stopped.

"Hey! I remember that you are very good at drawing flowers and butterflies. I'm not good at drawing those, but I need them right here. Can you draw them for me?"

"Of course Ben. I'd be happy to. After all, we used to draw together all the time." said Darla.

Darla and Ben kept on drawing and painting.

They did the meadows, the river, and the butterflies. They made beautiful drawings. They drew Eagle, who looked stunning among the other creatures in the woods.

They were so immersed in their drawings that they hardly noticed the time. It was almost dark when finally Darla said:

"We better go home now Ben. It's almost dark. Mom and dad will be worried if we don't get home soon. Besides, we have a lot to do at home. Don't forget, we will be leaving for Canada soon."

The time had finally arrived. The family left their home in the Philippines for the new life that awaited them in Canada. Everyone was very excited to go, but when they got there, it wasn't exactly what Darla had imagined.

Darla's first impression of Canada was that it was very windy and dreary. She noticed dead leaves scattered all over the ground. The sun was about to set in the west. Darla could already feel a chill approaching in the air. "It's beautiful in its own way but it's very cold and grey." Darla thought to herself. The cold and gloomy weather came as a shock to all of them, but especially to Darla.

They eventually arrived at Uncle Sam's house. Darla hoped to see Aunt Lucia and Christina waiting to greet them, but they were both working that night. Uncle Sam told Darla not to worry --- that they would be home in the morning.

"Hey Darla!" It was Ben's voice. "Don't just stand there. Help me with these bags. They are too heavy. I can't carry them by myself."

"Coming Ben." Darla ran to help. "Where are we going to put them Ben?" asked Darla.

"In the basement," replied Ben. "It's like an apartment. I heard Uncle Sam telling mom and dad that we can stay here until we get settled. Come on now. Let's get inside."

The next few days that followed were full of excitement. Uncle Sam and aunt Lucia showed them around the city. They were amazed with the tall buildings, the speeding cars, trucks and vans on the highways, and the beautiful toys and gorgeous clothes on display at shopping malls. They even went to see Christina, during one of her modeling sessions.

Then suddenly reality hit them. They had to adjust fast. Uncle Sam, and Aunt Lucia had to go back to work. What a mad rush to see them in the morning! Christina was also busy. She was taking ballet, piano, swimming lessons and other classes of which Darla couldn't remember them all.

"That's weird," she thought. "Christina has to take swimming lessons. Where I'm from, you don't take lessons. You just swim."

There was hardly any time to settle in. Mom and dad had to find jobs. Most of the time, Darla and Ben were left alone. They felt kind of lost. They couldn't even go out to play. Aunt Lucia told them not to go out on their own. It was too dangerous. There were lots of strangers around. Darla and Ben were so lonely. They got bored of watching T.V., and playing with the plastic toys Christina had given them. Slowly the joy and excitement of coming to Canada were fading away.

One day as Ben was looking for something to do, he came across one of the bags he brought with him from the Philippines.

"Hey Darla, look! I found our drawings. Aren't they beautiful? Look at this one. Eagle seems alive in there. Oh! How I miss him."

Eagerly, Darla looked at the drawings. She thought they were really beautiful. "Ben, I'm glad you brought these drawings with you. It's nice to see them again."

"Come, let's draw some more. I brought all our drawing and painting tools. We can start now if you want. We have nothing else to do anyway."

"Okay --- and let's show them to Uncle Sam, Aunt Lucia and Christina, when we're done."

That evening, after supper, Darla and Ben didn't waste any time. They promptly showed their drawings to the entire family. Everyone crowded around to see their lovely artwork.

"These are really beautiful." Uncle Sam and Aunt Lucia both said. "Did you do them all by yourselves?"

"We didn't realize, how good you were until now." commented mom and dad.

"Can I have a look?" Christina asked.

Christina looked at the drawings. She looked at the paintings too. She looked at them very closely. Darla and Ben both wondered why Christina seemed so captivated.

"Oh wow! These drawings and paintings are so beautiful. There is an art contest being sponsored by the store that I work for. If you want, I'll enter a few of them for you. What do you say?" asked Christina.

"Really?!" Darla and Ben got very excited. "That would be great! Do you really mean it? Do you really think that our drawings are good?"

"Of course I do." answered Christina with a smile. "Write both your names and address at the bottom. I'll be going to work tomorrow, so I can hand them in for you."

"Thanks Christina. That's very nice of you."

The following day was Darla and Ben's first day of school in Canada.

"Darla, Ben, wake up!" It was mom's voice. "School starts today. We have to be there early. Hurry now, have breakfast, then get changed." Mom was quite in a rush.

"What's for breakfast mom?" Ben asked.

"Toasted bread and chocolate milk. You could have jam or margarine with your bread if you like."

"Toasted bread again? Why can't we have fried rice, fish and banana like we used to have?" complained Ben. "Everyday, toasted bread. I'm sick and tired of it."

"Ben, must you complain like that? I promise I'll make something special on the weekend." Replied mom.

"I wish we were back in the Philippines. I miss Eagle and all my friends. We don't have many friends here. Besides, you and dad are hardly ever home."

Mom's face flushed. Her eyes watered. She rubbed her eyes and turned away from them both.

Darla was very quiet. She knew exactly how Ben felt. She felt the same too, but she didn't say a word. She looked thoughtfully at her mom. Darla knew that mom was crying. She felt sorry for her. This change of life was hard on all of them.

"Mom, where is dad?" she asked.

"He left with Uncle Sam. Uncle Sam said there is a job opening where he works. He told dad it's worth trying." Mom took a deep breath, then--------

"We better get going, kids. I only took a half-day off work. I have to be back by one o'clock." And off they went.

At school, Darla and Ben were both very nervous. Although their teachers seemed very nice and friendly, Darla and Ben couldn't help but feel shy and out-of-place.

There were a lot of rules that Darla and Ben were not used to. They both tried to be on their best behavior and to be very attentive to their teachers and their lessons.

At recess, the children asked Darla and Ben so many questions.

Sometimes, they laughed at their answers.

They laughed at their accents too.

Some kids were mean, especially a girl named Ruby and a boy named Arnold, who was around Ben's age.

Ruby and Arnold kept laughing and whispering things to each other. It was clear that they were making fun of Darla and Ben.

Darla felt humiliated and her face began to turn red. Ben clenched his fist. He was getting upset, but Darla pulled him aside and tried to calm him down.

"Let's go Ben," Darla said as she lead him to the other side of the playground.

As they were walking, two children approached them.

"Hi." both of the children said at once.

"Hi." Darla and Ben answered shyly.

"My name is Carmen and this is my brother Tom. We haven't seen you before. Are you new to this school?"

"Yes, we just came here about two weeks ago." Darla replied.

"Where do you live?" asked Carmen.

"We are staying at my uncle Sam's house, not too far from here. How about you? Where do you live?"

"Not to far from the school either. Who knows, we might be neighbors. That would be great if we were!"

R-i-n-g   r-i-n-g   r-i-n-g   r-i-n-g   r-i-n-g   r-i-n-g

"There goes the bell. We better get to class." said Tom, and off they went. Darla and Ben both thought Carmen and Tom were very nice and hoped that they would become friends.

As winter approached the days went by faster. It was getting colder outside. The trees were nearly bare.

The kids at school still laughed at Darla and Ben. Everything they did seemed wrong to the other kids. Everything they said sounded funny to them as well.

Darla and Ben lost interest in school. They didn't want to go anymore. However, their parents would not allow them to miss their classes. They reminded Darla and Ben that a good education is a very important thing.

One Friday morning Darla woke up in a happy mood. "Tomorrow is Saturday," she thought. "Only one more day of school before the weekend."

That day Darla's class was learning about how to tell time. Her teacher put the long hand of the classroom clock at two and the short hand at ten, then asked ---

"Darla, what time is it?"

Without hesitation, Darla stood up. She had always been good at telling time.

"It's ten - ten ma'am."

The class roared with laughter.

Darla was confused and embarrassed. Her face turned a bright red. She started screaming "What's wrong? What's so funny? Look at the time. The long hand is pointing at two, and the short hand is pointing at ten, so it *is* ten-ten"

The class laughed even louder. The teacher tried to calm the class down, but it took a while before the laughter subsided.

"It's not ten- ten, Darla. It's ten *past* ten." said Ruby in a nasty tone.

Darla stormed out of the classroom. She didn't even ask permission. Her heart was broken. She never felt so out of place.

She ran to the washroom. For a long time she cried. She cried and cried, until she couldn't cry anymore. She wished she could go home to mom, but she knew her mother wouldn't be home until the evening.

That night, Darla had a dream.

It was a pleasant dream in the beginning, but it quickly turned scary.

In her dream, Darla saw herself in a creepy old forest. She was running from something that she could not see. It was getting dark. She could not find her way out. She stopped and looked all around. There were lots of big old trees.

To Darla, it appeared as though the trees had faces: mouths that seemed to sneer at her --- eyes that scowled at her --- and arms that reached out for her. Darla felt as if the trees were closing in all around her. As they moved, she thought she could hear them mocking her.

She started to run again. She ran for what seemed like miles without any sense of direction. She was very scared. She didn't know where to go or whom to turn to. Suddenly she saw a crowd of children. They were wearing different types of clothes and joyfully holding hands in circle. They were singing and dancing. Screaming, Darla ran to them, hoping desperately that they could help her out of this dreadful forest. When suddenly-----

"Darla! Darla! wake up." It was mom, gently shaking her.

Darla opened her eyes. She was sweating and shaking. "Mom, oh, mom!" Darla buried her face on her mother.

"It's okay." mom said in a soothing voice. She embraced her and stroked her hair to calm her down. "I'm here. You're safe. It's okay. It was only a dream. It must have been a very bad dream."

After Darla had settled down mom said: "I have some good news. Dad got the job. He will start on Monday. It won't be long until we find our own place." Mom was smiling gently as she told Darla the good news.

"That is great news, Mom." replied Darla. Her face brightened up. "What kind of job?"

"I think it is a maintenance job. I'm not really sure. The important thing is that he got the job."

"There's another thing," remarked mom. "Two children came looking for you, last night. You went to bed so early that you missed them. They said that they go to the same school as you. They live around here too, just four houses down from here."

"Did you get their names mom?" Darla asked eagerly.

"Yes, Carmen and Tom. They seem to be very nice."

"They are nice mom." Darla closed her eyes. She thought of Carmen and Tom. She thought of her dream too; the crowd of children dancing and singing. She felt relieved. "Well," said mom. "It's almost morning. I'm going to start making breakfast." And off she went.

Darla looked at the window. The sun was rising. The rays were beautiful. The birds were chirping happily. Darla's heart felt light.

Suddenly, she heard Christina and Ben's voice. It sounded like they were walking over to her room. Soon they were knocking at the door.

"Come in." Darla answered.

In walked Christina and Ben. They both appeared to be very excited.

"What is it Christina? What is it Ben? You two look like you have something very important to say."

"Christina said she has a surprise for us, but she won't tell me what it is," replied Ben. "Ok Christina, Darla is here too…so what is the big surprise?"

"Darla, Ben, you won't believe it!" announced Christina. "Do you remember the drawings that you two did? The drawings that I entered in the contest?"

"Yes, what about them?" Darla and Ben asked eagerly, their eyes widening. "Did they think our drawings were good?" Darla and Ben were both very excited. Their hearts were beating fast.

"Of course they did! You won second place! They told me that your drawing with the horses was really excellent, almost as good as the one that was awarded first prize. They said if you keep practicing you could easily win first place."

"Oh wow! That is terrific!" Darla and Ben embraced each other. They were so happy.

"Here is your prize and a certificate stating that you were a second place winner. It was even signed by our store manager. Imagine that." Christina handed them the envelope and the certificate.

"Thanks Christina. You're the best!"

Darla and Ben looked at the certificate. They looked at it for a long time. Then they opened the envelope. Their eyes widened in disbelief. Inside the envelope were two one-hundred dollar bills. They could hardly believe their eyes.

For a while, they were both speechless. Finally they came around and at that moment they held each other tight. Then they hugged Christina. When both of them settled down, they said---

"Thank you again Christina. You really made our day." and they both hugged her again.

"Hey, no problem. But if you really want to thank me, then how about taking me out on a shopping spree?" joked Christina.

"Oh yes, of course! Where do you want us to take you?" replied Darla and Ben, beaming with joy.

"Hey, don't take me seriously. I'm just teasing the two of you. Use the money to buy something you will both enjoy."

"Christina, you really are the best!" They hugged her once more.

"It was my pleasure." said Christina. "Don't forget to show your certificate to Uncle Sam and Aunt Lucia. I'm sure, they will be glad to see your great accomplishment."

"We will!" answered Darla and Ben.

Darla thought for a moment about all the good fortune that had come their way this morning. She felt very happy and very blessed.

"I think it would be a good idea if we show our certificate and artwork to the class on Monday during 'Show and Tell.' I think that all the kids will be very impressed with what we've accomplished. And maybe, just maybe, after they see this certificate, they'll stop laughing at us. What do you think Ben?"

"I think that's a terrific idea Darla, but what about the money? Certainly we can't just keep it for ourselves." Replied Ben

"Of course not. We should give the money to mom and dad --- to help out --- Besides, they would know how to use it better than us."

"Great! Let's go!" exclaimed Ben.

And with a renewed sense of hope and determination, they happily left the room.

The End